THE RISK FREE BINARY OPTIONS STRATERGY

    I am going to show you how to double your money every 5 days RISK FREE weather you start with $10 dollars or $200

Every binary option product in the market will say "$300 in 60 seconds", Or "$1000 in an hour", but no one talks about the consistency of these earnings. You can lose $300 in 60 seconds also.

Without proper knowledge of the market and trading, you may win occasionally, but over time you will face losses. Binary Options is not simply guessing whether the market will be up or down after certain time.

If you don't have an edge it's the same as betting on red or black at roulette 50-50. You could have a run of 3-4 wins and then have a run of 10 losses.

I am going to show you a strategy which keeps things simple for traders new to binary's *and* reduces the chances of losses and hence reduces the risk. With my strategy, the probability of winning 98% of the time is a reality.

INTRODUCING THE RISK FREE BINARY OPTIONS STRATEGY

This ultra-low risk strategy is based on the binary option touch trade and is used in conjunction with the *BETONMARKETS* platform.
This is because they have a unique feature which allows you to select your barrier position and expiry time when placing a trade. No other broker offers this feature on touch/no touch trading which is essential for this strategy to work.
***BETONMARKETS** is a well-established broker who has been in business since 1999 and is respected throughout the industry.*

Also *BETONMARKETS* offer a free demo account with no strings so you can practice fine tuning the strategy for as long as you want. No other brokers offers this.

If you have problems opening an account with BETONMARKETS never fear. I have a backup Binary Broker *24OPTION.COM.* The strategy can be applied using this broker although the touch option does not have the flexibility of BETONMARKETS but you can set the expiry time much shorter and adjust your stake to achieve the same result. The important thing is the TECHNICAL ANALYSIS that you do beforehand which is the same.
Also *24OPTION.COM* will require a small deposit before you open a free DEMO account But after that you can practice away. . This Broker is fully regulated.

FINDING THE TRADE

The essence of the forex risk free touch strategy is finding a currency pair that is trending up or down and placing a trade 8-20 pips away from the spot price. The closer your trade is to the spot price the lower the return BUT the probability of the price touching the bar in the direction of the trend so close to the spot price becomes almost certain(with some added safeguards that I will talk about later)

For example EUR/USD is trending upwards on the 5min and 60min time frames. Its spot price 1.3082. You decide on a 15% return and place a trade at 1.3090 touch. Usually within a few minutes the trade will expire (the trade will stay live for 1 day in the event of it taking longer so don't panic).

As the trade expires you have an easy $15.usualy after a few minutes Not much you say compared to 60 sec binary trading. If you can win consistently with 60 sec binary trading with all the stress and potential for loss that entails then this is not for you.

If on the other hand if you do the above 9 or 10 times each day 5 days a week, You will make $750 per week from your initial $100 stake doubling up every 2 weeks will make you $4000 after about a month depending on how many trades you can make. I have done this already. And this was with a 10% return only.

If your appetite for risk is a little greater you can set the bar 10-20 pips away from the spot price for $25-$40 return per trade **if the market is trending sharply on the lower time frames. This will return $250 /day min**

Right now I am going to take you through the process in detail and we are going to make a trade that will return $20 on a $100 stake with no risk. Just follow the steps I am going to show you.

Firstly you will need a free copy of **METATRADER 4**. Just open a demo account with any broker (I personally use HOTFOREX) but any one will do, and download it to your PC.

Click on "NEW CHART" in top left hand corner. See below screenshot and read the following if you are unfamiliar with MT4 Check this guide.
METATRADER 4 GUIDE

Open 4 major pairs EUR/USD GBP/USD   EUR/GB USD/CHF and check the 4 hour chart. Then add a 60 simple moving average to each chart to establish the general trend. See picture 1 (I WILL USE EU/USD FOR ALL EXAMPLES)

THE EUR/USD 4 HOUR CHART IN UPTREND.

FIND YOUR PAIRS

When you have found 2-3 pairs trending up or down on the 4 hour chart go to the free site INVESTING.COM and find the forex pairs page. This great site gives you free technical analysis over 4 time frames using indicators, moving averages and a summary For each pair.

LOOK FOR 3 BUYS orSTRONG BUYS   or 3SELLSorSTRONG SELLS IN THE SUMMARY ROW THAT COMPLIMENTS YOUR METATRADER 4 TRENDS.
AS ABOVE. BUT MAKE SURE IT'S AT LEAST 3 REDS OR 3 GREENS. 2 IS NOT GOOD ENOUGH.

When you find 3 in a row open up the more detailed window for the pair (below) and check the short term movement on the 15 min chart. It will be fluctuating but you know the main trend so if the main trend is up you wait until the 15 min chart is retracing from a down fluctuation and have your BETONMARKETS site open at TOUCH/NO-TOUCH page. See below

Note the EUR/USD Summary ie 4 strong buy signals-You can really go to town on this one and make 8-10 trades that will mature in a few minutes and then jump in again, and again.

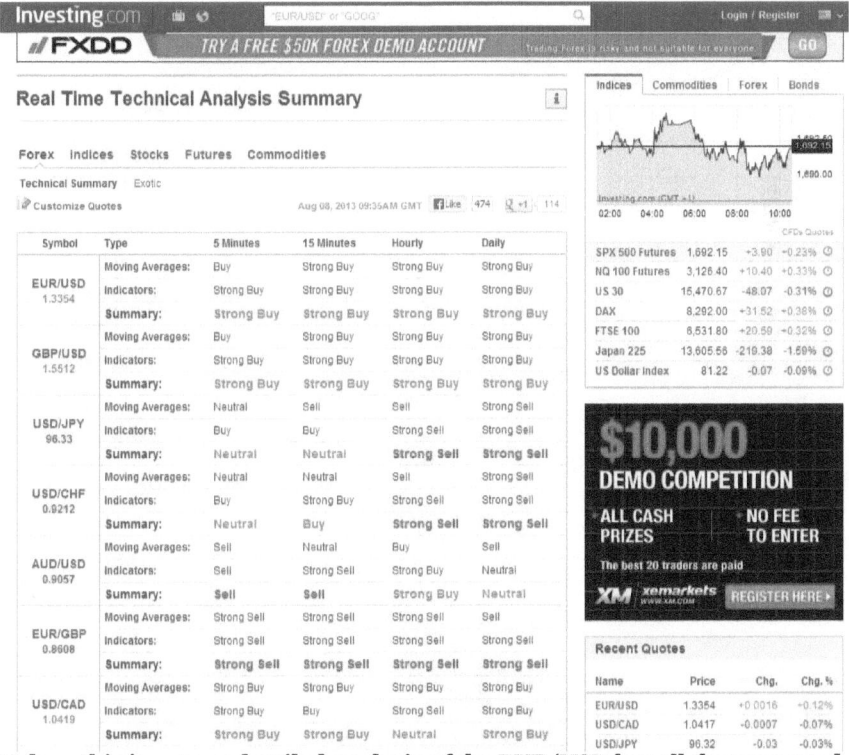

Below this is a more detailed analysis of the EUR/USD but all that you need to make your trade is in the real time analysis summary.

▼ **1.3071** -0.0029 (-0.22%)

⏱ 12:12:48 GMT - Real-time Data (Disclaimer)

Type: Currency
Group: Major
Base: Euro
Second: US Dollar

Prev. Close **1.3099** | Bid/Ask **1.3069 / 1.3072** | Day's Range **1.3056 - 1.3120**

General | **Chart** | **Technical** | **News & Analysis** | **Community** | **Brokers**

Technical Analysis | Candlestick Patterns | Forex Systems

EUR/USD Technical Analysis

👍 Like 6   +1

5 mins | 15 mins | 30 mins | Hourly | 5 Hours | **Daily**

Summary:	BUY			
Moving Averages:	STRONG BUY	Buy (11)	Sell (1)	
Technical Indicators:	NEUTRAL	Buy (3)	Sell (3)	

Pivot Points »   Apr 30, 2013 12:12PM GMT

Name	S3	S2	S1	Pivot Points	R1	R2	R3
Classic	1.2962	1.2997	1.3046	1.3081	1.3130	1.3165	1.3214
Fibonacci	1.2997	1.3029	1.3049	1.3081	1.3113	1.3133	1.3165
Camarilla	1.3071	1.3079	1.3086	1.3081	1.3102	1.3109	1.3117
Woodie's	1.2968	1.3000	1.3052	1.3084	1.3136	1.3168	1.3220
DeMark's	-	-	1.3063	1.3090	1.3147	-	-

Technical Indicators »   Apr 30, 2013 12:12PM GMT

Symbol	Value	Action
RSI(14)	54.300	Neutral
STOCH(9,6)	45.870	Neutral
STOCHRSI(14)	44.828	Sell
MACD(12,26)	0.001	Buy
ADX(14)	14.711	Neutral
Williams %R	-51.837	Neutral
CCI(14)	65.3944	Buy
ATR(14)	0.0089	Less Volatility

Moving Averages »   Apr 30, 2013 12:12PM GMT

Period	Simple	Exponential
MA5	1.3049 Buy	1.3060 Buy
MA10	1.3042 Buy	1.3055 Buy
MA20	1.3061 Buy	1.3032 Buy
MA50	1.2988 Buy	1.3052 Buy

		1,589.00	
		1,587.00	
		1,586.45	

Investing.com (GMT -1)
04:00 06:00 08:00 10:00 12:00

CFDs Quotes

SPX 500 Futures	1586.45	-1.80	-0.11%	
NQ 100 Futures	2858.70	-0.05	0.00%	
US 30	14818.83	+106.26	+0.72%	
DAX	7916.50	+43.00	+0.55%	
FTSE 100	6448.30	-9.72	-0.15%	
Japan 225	13860.86	-23.27	-0.17%	
US Dollar Index	82.24	+0.08	+0.10%	

Top Financial Analysts

BANC DE BINARY   STAR TRADING

Recent Quotes | My Portfolio

Name	Price	Chg.	Chg. %
GBP/USD	1.5481	-0.0020	-0.13%
USD/JPY	97.44	-0.34	-0.34%
USD/CAD	1.0112	-0.0003	-0.02%
EUR/JPY	127.38	-0.70	-0.55%
EUR/USD	1.3071	-0.0029	-0.22%

🗑 Clear all recent quotes

EUR/USD 11:25:02
L: 1.30476 2.6 H: 1.30923

Trading the Euro can be

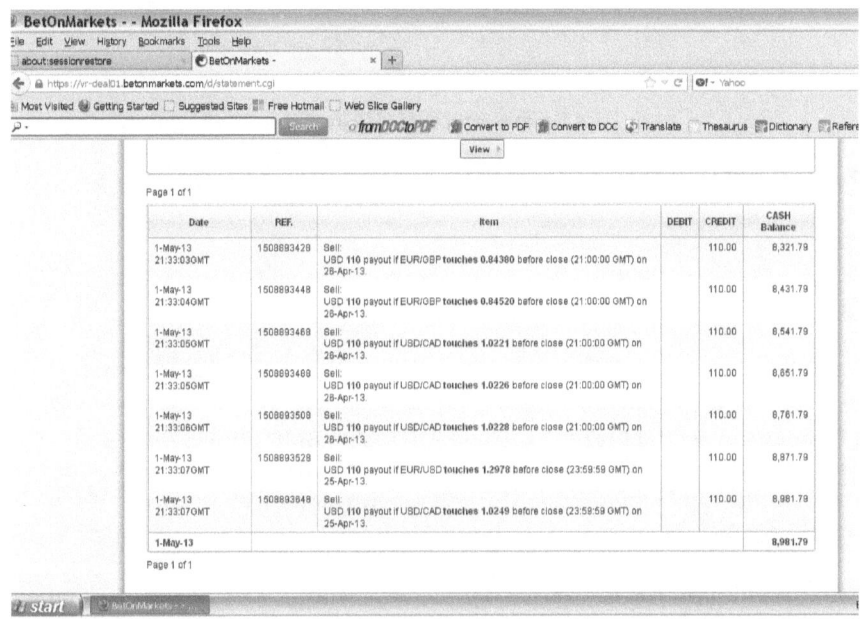

The above is a list of trades I made one afternoon in about one hour after finding 3 trending pairs. This can be done over and over again any time of day although the best time is during the London and New York sessions as they tend to yield bigger movements. Please note this was a very conservative 10% return in a very strong trending market. I could have gone for 20 or 30% in this market and still made 100% winning trades.
Look out for news items that affect the market like "the non-farming payroll figures" or the "BANK OF ENGLAND INTEREST STATEMENT" monthly news items that can trigger massive moves in the EUR/USD and GBP/USD markets. Just Google FOREX NEWS ITEMS and bookmark the site that suits you and make a note of the dates.

LEARNING TOUCH OPTIONS

Touch Options

Go to Start Betting -> Touch/No Touch

Ignore the No-touch option as we will not be needing that.

You can select the market and it will show you the Current spot of that market. Then you can input a barrier and duration for which you want to place a trade. 0 days means the trade will expire at the end of the day. (For Touch Options, 0 days is available only for Random Indices.) The payout refers to the total amount that you will receive along with the profit if you win the trade.

Once you hit the "Get Bet Prices" button, you will get 2 trade options on the right. In the above example,

As you make the barrier closer to the current spot, the Return percentage for Touch option decreases. Play around with these variables until you are comfortable with the results. It's a bit tricky at first but you will soon get the hang of it.

You can also see the trend graph at the bottom of the page. The blue line shows the selected barrier. You can select 1 hour, 6 hours, and 12 hours trend up to 365 days. The below graph shows the trend of last 6 hours. If you select the Interactive Charts option, you can also see the more interactive candlestick chart you will see the Bet Details, your Purchase Price and the Current Market Price of your trade. Current Market Price is decided by the current state of your trade i.e. the time left and the closeness to the barrier.

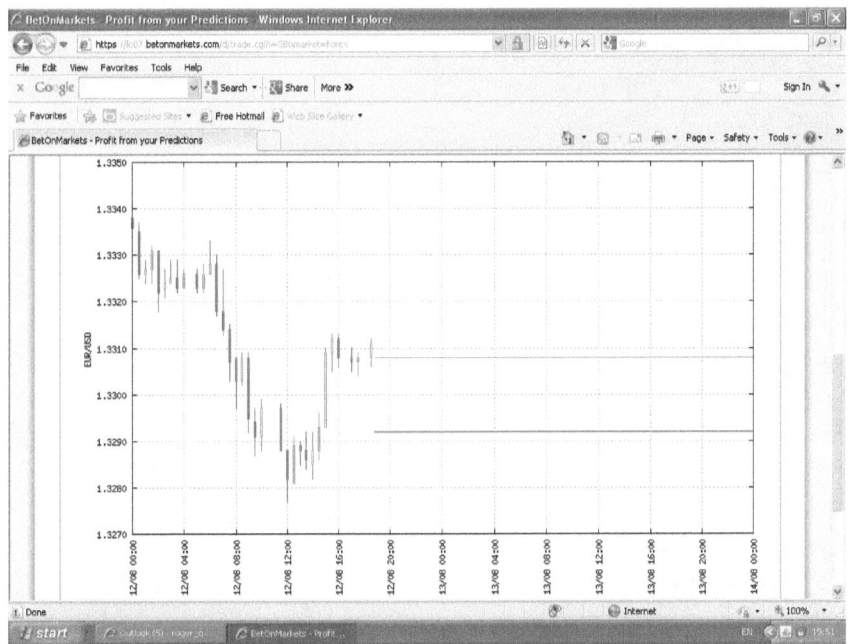

This Chart shows the position of your bar(blue line) and the spot price (grey line)
When it hits the blue bar you have won even if it retraces it only has to touch once
And you have won. The candle stick chart below gives a more informative picture
Of the price action. You can see the open, close and direction over the time frame
But the trend is still very obviously down.

This is the interactive candle stick chart similar to MT4 charts

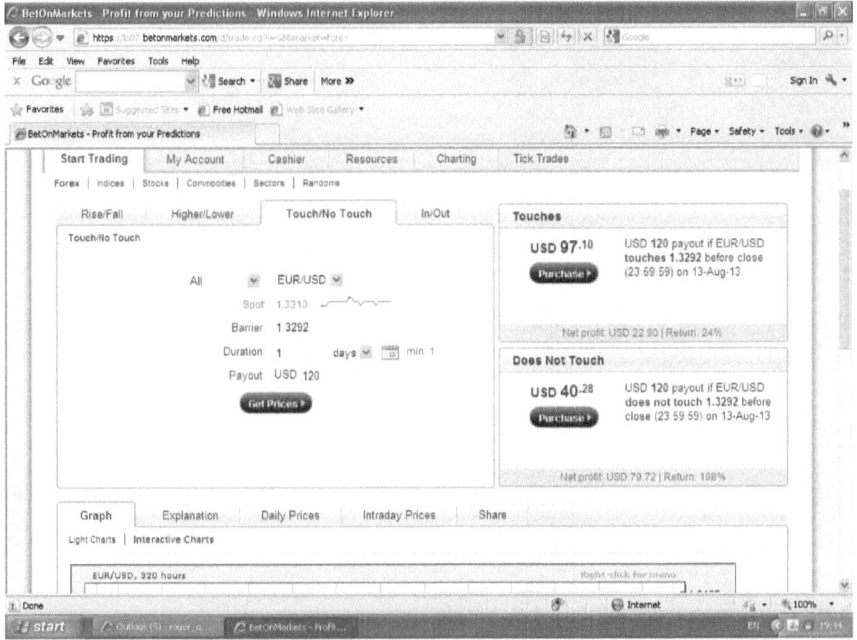

The price only needs to move 18 pips in your favor in the downward trend for you to win. This can happen in minutes in a trending market but can sometimes take an hour or 2. If you have done the analysis using **INVESTING.COM** you will win every time. If on the rare occasions that a trade reverses against you for instance because of some economic news that affects the market you can sell your trade before expiration—a great help in minimizing losses.

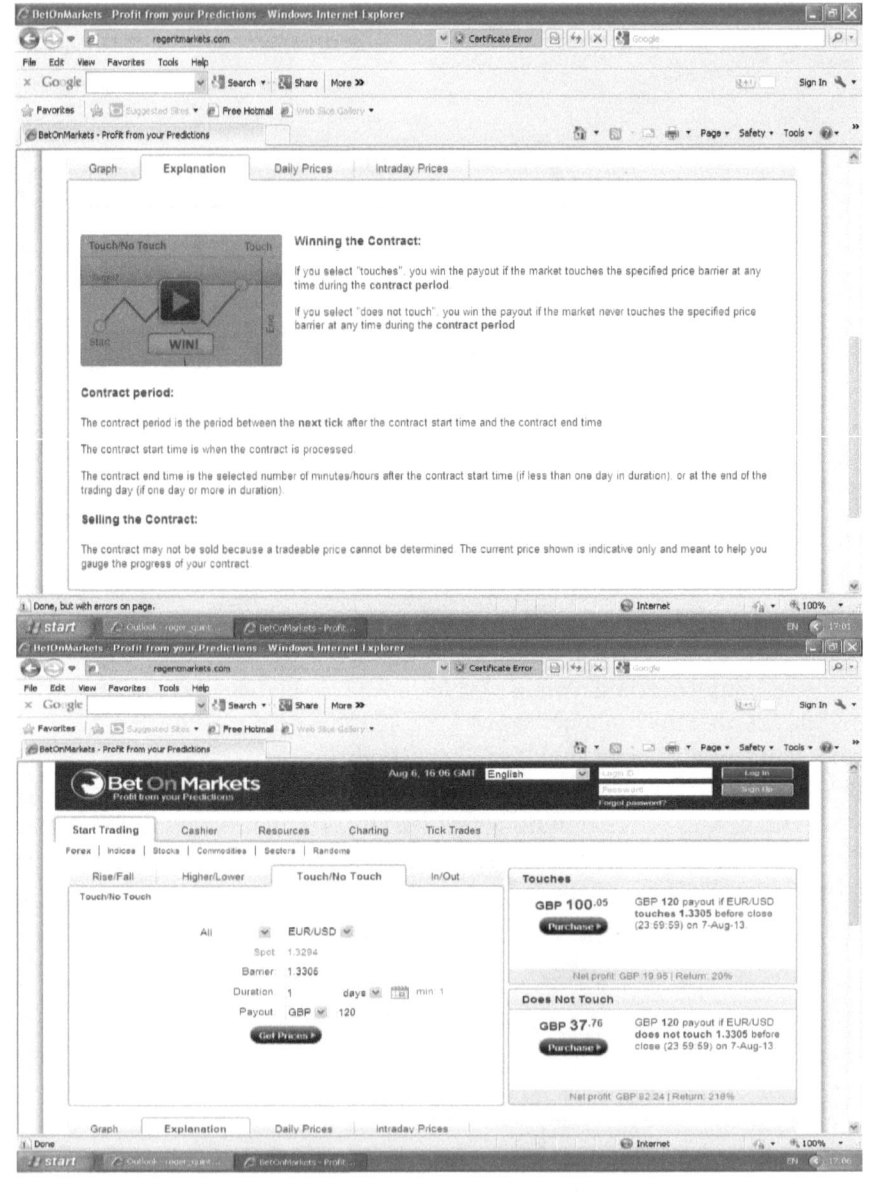

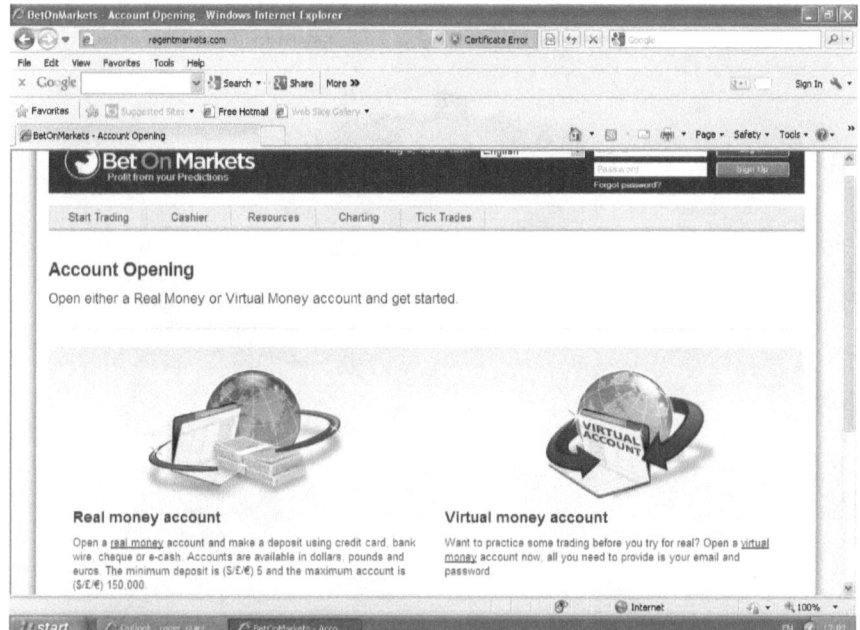

So get to it and open your free DEMO account with BETONMARKETS now and start practicing and perfecting your technique. When you are confident open a real money account and start with small stakes of say $20 untill your confidence grows.

Thank you for reading my little strategy and good luck with your binary trading. I am now going to open your eyes to the wider FOREX picture which will get you on the road to forex trading proper. It's a vast subject and you are looking to learn all you can but one step at a time is the key. The forex resources I am about to show you are the result of 5 years research learning and testing. Everything I am showing you I have used myself and made money with over that period. I have only included the sucesses.

Good Luck   Roger Q

FOREX RESOURCES

I am going to share with you some of the best forex resources on the planet that I have used over the last 5 years

Firstly for the basics of <u>FOREX TRADING</u> Go to this site which is free to all.

Next try the FREE <u>3 ducks system</u> by Captain Currency. Andy has a fun site and great system for beginners Plus 1 to 1 training which I have tried. I have no affiliation with the above sites I just belive they are a great place to start.

How would you like to be paid to trade? Yes really. You make money on every trade you make ----WIN or LOSE Its true, find out <u>HERE</u>

FOREX ROBOTS or EA's

Aside from my manual trading I have been trading with a number of robots over the past 5 years. I have purchased and tested about 50 all together but only these 4 have made me consistant money over this period.

I will list them in no particular order as they are all different. Some are short term scalpers some are medium term swing traders and some are long term. Used together they cover all market conditions.

I will give a brief description of each with a link to their site

MILLION DOLLAR PIPS .This is a robot developed by William Morrison It's a MEGA SCALPER that trades spikes in the market and has been very successful at what it does. Find out more HERE

FAPTURBO . This is the most well established robot for the past 5 years and can still double your money in 4 months. how? Find out HERE

MEGADROID. This one uses AI (artificial intelligence) and is a spectacular Success story. It worked for me consistantly over 6 months without loss. It can for you too. Try it HERE

PIPJET. This is another super scalper that achieves amazing results in no time at all.Get it HERE

When you have your trading account and robots set up how would you like to make $20000 per month using a very small trading capital?

Yes its possible and you are one step away from this incredible little known Method of levering your forex income to unimagined levels find out now

Keep an eye on my website for new Forex articles and information and good luck with your FOREX trading.
                        Roger Q

These are not trade recommendations. This information is best used with discretion in addition with your own market analysis and trading ideas. I do not accept liability for any loss or damage, including without limitation to any loss of profit which may arise directly or indirectly from use or reliance on such information.

C Roger Quinton

Binary Options: A Brief History & Overview

Binary options are quickly becoming a favourite of traders as both a hedging and speculation tool. While they seem relatively new, binary options have been traded for well over a decade, though they were originally traded over the counter usually between two institutional investors, mostly hedge funds and investment banking prop desks. Retail traders had to wait until 2008 before they were granted the right to trade binary options, and since then the popularity of this asset class has gone through the roof. But what exactly are binary options and how do they work? Let's take a look:

Binary options can best be summed up as a trade that offers only two distinct outcomes, either your trade finishes in the money (winner) or out of the money (loser). This is in stark contrast to traditional vanilla options where concepts such as time decay (theta), volatility, strike price, time to expiration and the like all go into the pricing. Binary options offer a simple risk-reward proposition, which is known and clearly stated prior to entering the trade. A lot of the trading sites that offer binary options place a return percentage of anywhere between 60% to 90% for winning trades and a 0% to 15% return of capital for losing trades.

Binary options are usually offered on a variety of underlying assets across most trading platforms. Stocks (otherwise known as equities) are offered across most platforms, but usually the number of stocks is limited. Stock binary options are typically only offered on the largest, most liquid names such as Apple, Google, Microsoft, Intel, JP Morgan, and the like. Technology stocks make up the majority of stock based binary options. Foreign exchange (forex) binary options are also well represented across platforms with most major currency pairs making up the bulk of trading. Popular commodities such as Gold, Silver, Oil, Natural Gas, and Copper and Major Indexes across the globe can also be found on most binary options trading platforms.

One common misconception about binary options revolves around expirations. Most people believe all binary options have a one-hour expiration time; this simply is not true. Over the past few years we've seen expirations range anywhere between 15 minutes on the low end all the way up to one month. While I don't know many people e frame and simplified payout structure so you are likely to see traders gravitate more to the one-hour binary options.

Binary Options Strategies Exposed

Binary options strategies come in all shapes and sizes but when you really take a closer look there are really just two overriding themes, speculation and hedging. In the following paragraphs we explore the most common speculation and hedging strategies used in binary options trading today.

Speculative Binary Options Strategies

Speculative binary options strategies typically consists of a trader implementing a some sort of technical analysis to pick high probability binary options entry points. Candlestick charts are used pretty extensively in these types of binary options strategies as they are pretty adept at identifying short-term trends, something all binary options traders strive for. When implementing speculative binary options strategies, traders tend to wait until the last few minutes prior to the lock out period to place a trade. Waiting until the last minute to place the binary trade minimizes the amount of time the trader needs to be correct in his/her short term directional choice. Stocks tend to move around a bit and it is very common for trends to reverse after a few minutes, so the shorter amount of time the trade is exposed the better for speculative binary options strategies traders.

Hedging Binary Options Strategies

On the extreme opposite end of speculation lie the hedging binary options strategies. While the speculative traders take on massive all or nothing risk in their trading activities, hedgers prefer to place a trade early in the expiration cycle, monitor the performance, and then decide on an appropriate action plan to ensure maximum gain and minimum loss. Hedgers usually implement one of three strategies during the expiration cycle. 1) Purchase a binary call (put) option early in the hour and, if the stock moves in the appropriate direction, purchase the opposite binary put (call) to lock in a profit zone and minimize the amount of downside risk. 2) Purchase a binary call (put) option early in the hour and, if the stock moves in the appropriate direction, purchase another binary call (put) to essentially double the trade amount. 3) Purchase a binary call (put) option, and if the stock moves against them, quickly purchase the opposite binary put (call). This strategy essentially locks in a loss unless the hedger is able to place another trade to create a profit zone.

These binary options strategies are used extensively throughout the day by experienced binary options traders. While the speculative binary options strategies incur more risk, the reward is significantly high enough that most traders of binary options end up using it the most. If you are more conservative then you should definitely consider going the hedging route.

Binary Trading Platforms

Your binary trading platform choice plays a critical part of your ultimate success as a binary options trader. While they may look the same, each binary trading platform is definitely not the same. Speed is essential in any trading activity, especially when the difference between winning huge and losing big is a mere fraction of a penny apart. That's why it's important to get comfortable with the defining characteristics of your binary trading platform of choice as quickly as possible. See appendix for recommended Brokers

Binary Trading Platform Charting Capabilities

Each platform provides some sort of charting functionality so you can easily see graphically where you are placing your trades. Some charts on the various platforms are better than others. Make sure you pick a binary trading platform that has real time graphs that can easily be seen next to the trade entry area. While this seems like a no-brainer, do not overlook this seemingly minor point. Remember how we said speed is everything, well the difference between using a binary trading platform chart and using an independent chart outside of the platform can cause you to miss a potential trade by seconds, time that could be critical in determining a winning trade and losing trade. I learned the hard way. When I first started trading binary options I used independent charting sources to determine my entry points. After losing a few trades by 0.0002 cents (seriously!) I decided I couldn't risk the time that it took to look back and forth and miss a solid trading opportunity.

Binary Trading Platform Order Entry

Another seemingly minor point here but do not underestimate the importance of selecting a platform that is easy to switch between purchasing a put or call. I also learned this one the hard way (see a pattern here!) A lot of times you will find yourself switching back and forth between puts and calls, especially when a pattern is at a critical juncture that could yield a quick breakout or strong reversal. Make sure your binary trading platform of choice switches easily and quickly between puts and calls because if there is a significant lag you may find yourself purchasing a binary call when you meant to purchase a binary put. There is nothing worse than reading the charts correctly, placing a trade based on your reading, then realizing you selected the wrong put or call by accident. Remember this is binary options trading, there are no re-dos, no mulligan's, and you have to live with your decisions even if they were made in error. So take some time to get comfortable with the order entry functionality of your favourite binary trading platform, it could mean the difference between an exhilarating win and a crushing defeat.

Forex Binary Options Trading vs. Traditional Forex Trading

Forex binary options are slowly but surely starting to gain in popularity amongst traditional forex traders. Why you ask? Because forex binary options present several advantages to traders that simply can not be duplicated in traditional forex trading. Let's take a look:

Expiration Benefits of Forex Binary Options

Forex binary options typically expire every hour. While this may not seem like a big advantage to some, a disciplined trader can truly appreciate this benefit. Instead of placing stop-loss orders and/or waiting for the position to reach a certain level before exiting, forex binary options either incur a gain or loss every hour. No need to worry about 2 hour or daily performance, one hour gets you in and out.

Risk Management Benefits of Forex Binary Options

The moment you place a forex binary options trade you immediately know the maximum potential gain and maximum potential loss of the trade. Even if you combine a few forex binary options trades together, it is very easy to determine how much capital you are placing at risk and the potential reward for this risk. This is a huge advantage over traditional forex trading which doesn't inherently have a risk management component and requires careful monitoring in order to efficiently and effectively manage risk. Actually traditional forex trading in some ways is exactly the opposite of forex binary options trading from a risk management perspective, in the sense that extreme leverage increases the risk of a position blowing up your whole portfolio!

Binary Options + Forex Trading = Win-Win Scenario

Smart forex traders recognize the benefits including forex binary options in their portfolio can have on overall performance. So what you are seeing is a growing number of traders using forex binary options to hedge their positions. Instead of panicking when a forex position starts to move against you, consider placing an appropriately sized forex binary options trade in the new direction of the underlying. Because of the large return characteristics inherent in binary options in many instances an appropriately hedged forex position can yield a profit no matter what direction the underlying moves once the forex binary options position is established.

This is the new paradigm shift in forex trading. You are exposing yourself to too much risk and possibly even limiting your profit potential if you are not including forex binary options in your trading activities. So find a solid binary options trading platform and start implementing a disciplined hedging strategy today that can save you money.

How Often Should You Place A Binary Option Trade?

The answer to how often you should place a binary option trade is really determined by what kind of trader you are. Some people are very picky about placing a binary option trade and will only do so when conditions are ripe for their overall strategy. I think this kind of discipline helps new binary options traders significantly in minimizing potentially disastrous effects of overtrading. Pick a system you've either tested yourself or have purchased and believe in and only place a binary option trade when your system says so. This way you can easily determine whether the system you are using is goo in picking binary option trade entry points or not. Trading binary options is often an exhilarating activity, filled with emotional swings, being disciplined in your approach makes it a lot easier to handle these volatile times and is a great learning tool in how to handle pressure and adversity not only in binary option trading but in life in general.

The Classic Over-Trader

This is a trap many inexperienced traders fall into when they start trading binary options. While the goal may be to exhibit patience and discipline when deciding to place a binary option trade, oftentimes our emotions and ego get in the way and we start to place binary option trades based on a gut feeling. Some binary option traders do really well following their gut instinct at first but eventually things turn and they end up having to go back to the disciplined system they started off using. We see theses over trading tendencies most often amongst hedgers. While careful consideration is taken before placing the initial binary option trade early in the expiration cycle, all bets are off once the underlying asset has a chance to move around. Recall that there are times hedgers find themselves locked into a two trade position that guarantees a loss, albeit a small one. Well no one likes to lose right? So what you'll see is traders looking to turn a small loss into some sort of gain at the risk of losing even more. This is bad form. A discipline trader following a disciplined system knows there is no harm in taking small losses on positions. The goal is to live another day to place another binary option trade and this can not occur if you continue to over trade, placing risky trades to avoid small losses. Our advice, take the loss and move on to the next trade.

The Many Advantages of Binary Trading

Binary trading has taken the trading world by storm over the past few years as day traders who have been used to scalping miniscule returns for small stock movements can now generate returns up to 90% for these same small stock movements through binary trading.

In its most simple form binary trading is a direction based, win loss proposition. If the trader is correct in picking the direction of the underlying asset in a given time frame he/she will win a set percentage (typically between 60% and 90%), and if the trader is incorrect in picking the direction of the underlying stock in a given time frame he/she will lose anywhere between 85% and 100% of the trade. Keep in mind in binary trading the magnitude of the underlying asset move is meaningless, the direction is all that matters. This can best be described in an example:

For instance say a trader thinks the price of Google is going to rise over the next hour, he/she could purchase a binary call option expiring at the top of the hour, at Google's current price. If the binary call option was purchased with shares of Google trading at $600, the trader would generate the winning return percentage (60-90%) if shares finished anywhere above $600 upon expiration. So whether shares of Google finished at $600.01 or $699 the trader would only generate the specified winning percentage. This is the essence of binary trading.

So who is exactly using binary trading as part of their daily trading activities? We've seen the most binary trading activity from stock day traders and forex traders. The one thing successful stock and forex day traders have is the ability to forecast price movement over short time intervals. If this best describes you then you need to jump on the binary trading train as soon as possible. However, price speculation isn't the only way these successful stock and forex traders are incorporating binary trading into their trading activities, they are also using binary trading as a hedging instrument. What I mean by this is instead of closing out a trade that is going against them, they may first consider placing an appropriately sized binary trade in the opposite direction of the original trade to offset potential losses. This is a super effective way to mitigate downside portfolio risk. In many instances not only does an effective binary trading hedge limit risk but it also increases overall profitability. Now that's what I call a win-win scenario!

What Time Is Best To Trade Binary Options?

Unlike traditional day trading where you need decent market volatility to generate nice gains, binary options do not require a whole lot of movement to generate out-sized gains. So when is the best time to trade binary options...all the time! Ok, so maybe that's a little over the top but there are certain times during the day that are ideal to trade binary options, so let's go over 2 specific time frames.

Trading On the Market Open

This is a little tricky. Traders either strongly love or strongly hate trading on market open. Stocks move around with so much volatility that sometimes it feels like a crap shoot in picking an appropriate direction. Binary options brokers know the feeling as well so many don't allow you to trade binary options until a certain time has passed. These market open time frames range anywhere between 5 minutes all the way up to a half an hour. For those of you who like to see huge moves in binary option prices you may want to trade binary options as close to the open as possible. One advantage of trading close to the open is these huge moves which can place your trade firmly in the money within minutes of placing the trade. Conversely, the binary trade can move against you immediately, placing your trade firmly out of the money. However, always remember when you trade binary options you always have the ability (at least until the lock out period commences) of hedging your trade. So if the trade moves against you right away you can start to implement a hedging strategy that can, in some instances, completely negate the effects of the unwanted move. Just something to think about as you start to trade binary options.

Trading On the Market Close

While binary platforms may differ on what time they'll let you start to trade binary options on a daily basis, they all let you trade options into the close of the market. During the last hour of trading you will at times see different stock movement patterns emerge that allow smart binary options traders the ability to place high reward / low risk trades on prior to expiration. We've known traders that focus solely on these market close opportunities and have made a killing doing it. This does take a lot of patience though as some wait all day and end up not placing any trades, which can be a frustrating thing. While these setups do not occur everyday, it is best to learn them as you begin to trade binary options.

A Simple Binary Options Strategy

As a new binary options trader it is imperative to prepare yourself mentally and emotionally for the highs and lows that come along with binary trading. Hopefully you've taken the time to select a good binary options trading platform, one that is easy to use and fits your style of trading whether that be forex, stocks, commodities, or index trading. So now it's time to trade, where should you start. Well you know they say those who fail to plan, plan to fail. You need a solid binary options strategy. So that's what we have for you outlined below.

The Early Hedger Binary Options Strategy

The binary options strategy most newbie's use relies on a basic understanding of technical analysis. If you've never used any type of technical analysis to read charts, we suggest reading a book on candlestick charting, which seems to be the tool of choice of most binary traders. Incorporating candlestick charting into your binary options strategy will allow you to pick entry and exit points more efficiently. The dynamics of the early hedger binary options strategy can best be summarized as such:

1. Determine proper entry points for your binary option trade early in the expiration cycle (e.g. 10:00-10:15)

2. Allow the underlying time to make its move, closely monitoring opportunities to increase the size of the trade or hedge.

3. Start looking to place a potential second trade roughly 10 minutes prior to the lock out period

4. If the position is deep in the money your best bet is to probably leave it alone.

5. If the position is deep out of the money you can leave it alone and move on to the next trade or attempt to place 2 more trades to lock in a profit zone.

6. If the position is trading right around the initial entry point, you may want to consider placing the opposite binary trade position to limit maximum losses.

Follow these six steps to guide your initial trading actions. This early hedger binary options strategy is a sound way to control the potential

BINARY & FOREX RESOURCES

BETONMARKETS is a well-established broker who has been in business since 1999 and is respected throughout the industry.

Also **BETONMARKETS** offer a free demo account with no strings so you can practice fine tuning the strategy for as long as you want. No other brokers offers this.

I am going to share with you some of the best forex resources on the planet that I have used over the last 5 years

If you have problems opening an account with <u>BETONMARKETS</u> never fear. I have a backup Binary Broker <u>24OPTION.COM.</u> The strategy can be applied using this broker although the touch option does not have the flexibility of BETONMARKETS but you can set the expiry time much shorter and adjust your stake to achieve the same result. The important thing is the TECHNICAL ANALYSIS that you do beforehand which is the same.

Also <u>24OPTION.COM</u> will require a small deposit before you open a free DEMO account But after that you can practice away. . This Broker is fully regulated.

Firstly for the basics of <u>FOREX TRADING</u> Go to this site which is free to all.

Next try the FREE <u>3 ducks system</u> by Captain Currency. Andy has a fun site and great system for beginners Plus 1 to 1 training which I have tried. I have no affiliation with the above sites I just belive they are a great place to start.

How would you like to be paid to trade? Yes really. You make money on every trade you make ----WIN or LOSE Its true, find out <u>HERE</u>

FOREX ROBOTS or EA's

Aside from my manual trading I have been trading with a number of robots over the past 5 years. I have purchased and tested about 50 all together but only these 4 have made me consistant money over this period.

I will list them in no particular order as they are all different. Some are short term scalpers some are medium term swing traders and some are long term. Used together they cover all market conditions.

I will give a brief description of each with a link to their site

MILLION DOLLAR PIPS .This is a robot developed by William Morrison

It's a MEGA SCALPER that trades spikes in the market and has been very successful at what it does. Find out more HERE

FAPTURBO . This is the most well established robot for the past 5 years and can still double your money in 4 months. how? Find out HERE

MEGADROID. This one uses AI (artificial intelligence) and is a spectacular

Success story. It worked for me consistantly over 6 months without loss.

It can for you too. Try it HERE

PIPJET. This is another super scalper that achieves amazing results in no time at all.Get it HERE

When you have your trading account and robots set up how would you like to make $20000 per month using a very small trading capital?

Yes its possible and you are one step away from this incredible little known

Method of levering your forex income to unimagined levels find out now

Keep an eye on my website for new Forex articles and information and good luck with your FOREX trading.

_____ Roger Q

These are not trade recommendations. This information is best used with discretion in addition with your own market analysis and trading ideas. I do not accept liability for any loss or damage, including without limitation to any loss of profit which may arise directly or indirectly from use or reliance on such information.

Roger Quinton 2018

www.ingramcontent.com/pod-product-compliance
Lightning Source LLC
Chambersburg PA
CBHW031510210526
45463CB00008B/3172